Minimalist Budget:

The Ultimate Guide On How To Save Money & Do More With Less

William M. Thomas

ISBN: 171742242x
ISBN-13: 9781717422422

CONTENTS

Introduction

Thank you for taking the time to purchase this book: Minimalist Budget: The Ultimate Guide On How to Save Money & Do More With Less.

This book covers the topic of minimalist living and will teach you how to alter your current lifestyle to follow a more minimalist path and manage to live the best quality of life you can!

At the completion of this book you will have a good understanding of minimalist living and be able to budget accordingly to maintain a minimalist lifestyle, learn to be more frugal with your spending, and live your best life without feeling the need for material things!

Once again, thanks for purchasing this book, I hope you find it to be helpful!

What Is Minimalism?

You are awoken early by the latest iPhone, notifying you that it is time to get ready for the day. After your shower, you adorn yourself with designer clothes, slip on your designer shoes, and protect your eyes with an expensive pair of sunglasses. Off you go in this year's model car. Throughout the day, you are probably bombarded with advertisements asking you to purchase something. Most of these advertisements are not for something you need, but most people *will* buy these products. They feel they are living life to the maximum. Perhaps *you* are also part of this demographic!

We live in a culture of consumerism. We are constantly told buying more products will improve our quality life and bring us happiness. However, out of the madness of mass consumerism, a new trend is developing. This new trend emphasizes "less is more" and people who follow it strive to live their best life with as little as possible. This trend is called Minimalism.

You may have heard of Minimalism in a different context. You may think of it as an art form that depicts barren landscapes, monochromatic color schemes, and a few neatly-designed objects almost self-consciously placed in different corners of a room. You imagine that Minimalist living would be exactly this: having an empty space with few possessions. You may scoff at someone who is following a Minimalist lifestyle and imagine they have decided to shed their possessions to live as an ascetic. But I want you to stop worrying, because the Minimalist lifestyle as we know it today is none of these things!

Our lives are complicated; while some complications are inevitable, if we stop to reflect we will soon learn that many of our complications are self-inflicted. But when do we stop and reflect? We probably do not – and this is due to the fact that we are always busy and rushed, and do not have five minutes to spare for self-reflection; those five minutes are probably being spent in our endless chase for achieving happiness and living the perfect life. If you do find those five minutes to self-reflect, you will no doubt begin to wonder how your life got so complicated and what you can do to improve your conditions. You will notice that one of the biggest factors which is complicating your life is the chase and acquisition of material goods. You were probably under the impression that acquiring material goods was an indication of your personal and professional success; the more you own the more success you have attained seems to be the prevailing viewpoint. But before you know it, your standards continue to increase. Though you have acquired everything you once desired, they soon seem to lose their value and cause you more grief than joy. Yet you continue to believe that the only solution is to acquire more material goods. You no longer own these possessions – as a matter of fact, they now own you. You now realize that perhaps the answer is that less is more.

Minimalist living calls for discarding the unnecessary items you own and saving money by spending less. However, the point is not to lessen your quality of life and make you give up what you enjoy. Minimalist living is a way for you to enjoy life without needing to give in to the obsessive desire for pointless material things.

But how do you live a minimalist life? How do you get started? This book will help you answer these questions and offer you tricks for creating your own minimalist life.

Some of the tricks you will learn are:

- How to embrace the minimalist lifestyle
- How to discard unnecessary clutter
- Planning a budget
- Being frugal
- Prioritizing what you desire from life
- Carrying the minimalist approach to the digital world
- And more!

Before moving on, make sure you have a blank notebook and pen by your side. This book will contain action items; to utilize this book, it is best to follow these action items before advancing to the next section. I want to ensure that you are able to adopt a minimalist lifestyle and rather than simply reading about having one! This book is not intended to be read once and forgotten; rather, it works as a practical guide which you can continually reference to begin and continue your journey as a minimalist. This book aims to teach you how to live your best life, and I am certain if you follow the guidance provided, you will be living that life in no time..

Chapter One: The Minimalist Lifestyle

In this chapter, you will learn about the lifestyle that embraces minimalism and the different styles. Find out which one works for you!

The Internet is full of articles and videos regarding minimalism. Many individuals who embrace the minimalist lifestyle will list 150 things they own or 100 things they own. Many will live solely out of own suitcase or even a backpack! You will occasionally come across the adventurous individual who claims to possess nothing except for the shirt on their back! As a result, the person who owns 100 things may tell the person who owns 150 things that they are not following a minimalist lifestyle. This makes it feel like a competition to see who owns the fewest things.

But the minimalist lifestyle is not to be reduced to competition. You are choosing this lifestyle because you want to make the most out of life. Always keep that in mind as you prepare your lifestyle. Do not be swayed by the quantity of what you own; your lifestyle and commitment to minimalism is not defined by a number! As you read this book, keep in mind that this is a practical guide and the instructions are not to be taken as gospel. The minimalist lifestyle means something different for each individual, and the exercises and suggestions in this book are just that: suggestions. If something is not to your liking, it is not crucial to follow it, but keep in mind that the sole purpose of adopting this lifestyle is to live *deliberately* and get the most out of life with the *least*. Always remember this mantra as you decide what works for you and what does not.

Since minimalism has become a trending topic, it has been met with much skepticism. One of the most prevalent criticisms is that minimalism is only applicable for certain demographics. You must be single, earn a certain income, be a certain age, and live in a first world nation. Further criticisms in the American context have stated that it only works for white people. There is even a mindset that minimalism works for men but not for women. I want you to dispel all of these notions. If you truly want to, you can embrace minimalism.

Remember that not every aspect of minimalism will work for you. But you are not any less of a minimalist if you do not follow each aspect of the minimalist lifestyle. Based on your context, you decide what you can embrace. And remember, you can always try things later – you do not have to try everything at once. Minimalists are not born, they are made, slowly but surely! Adopting the minimalist lifestyle is to create a mindset for simplicity. We could all use a greater sense and appreciation for simplicity and contentment. Achieving this is feasible, no matter what your situation or context is.

As you embark upon your journey to adopting the minimalist lifestyle, here are a few things to keep in mind:

- Do not look down upon those who consume excessively simply because you have decided to cut down on your consumption.
- Do not kick yourself if it takes you a while to adopt any or all aspects of minimalist living suggested in this book; it is not a race!
- Focus on your minimalism before trying to rope others in to this lifestyle.
- Minimalism is an approach, not a religious doctrine with stringent rules. It is not that you must sell everything or live with the bare minimum. Embracing this lifestyle should train you to make measured decisions and live your life with a greater sense of awareness.
- Remember that your circumstances may change; there may be aspects of minimalist living which would be impractical for you to follow. You may own one suit which you hardly wear at present – but if you receive a senior

position at a multinational corporation, you will be expected to own a few more suits. This kind of minor alteration does not mean you have to forgo minimalism altogether. You will always have to analyze what aspects of your life can use the minimalist approach – do not worry, you will still be able to live life the minimalist way!

One important fact to remember is that the current approach to the minimalist lifestyle was born as a response to the excessive consumerism that pervades our society; however, it is not anti-shopping. Even if you go on a shopping spree every once in a while, you can still be a minimalist. The key is to own material goods that provide value and if you purchase more items, they should serve a function or have a long-term value.

You recall I suggested having a notebook and pen handy while reading this book? Now is the time to pull those things out.

Take a cursory glance over what you own and determine what provides value and what does not. For now, you do not need to list everything or go into grave detail. This exercise is a precursor to adopting a minimalist lifestyle. Pick a random sample of 20, 30, or even 50 items and determine which items have a strong value in your life and were worth the purchase. Was the guitar worth the purchase? Of course! It provides great music and exercises your mind. What about the Santa Claus statuette that's in a box gathering dust in the attic? It only needs to be taken out at Christmas, and even then, it does not *need* to be taken out. What about the lamp on the bedside table? Surely it serves a purpose. But, you could turn on the full light in the room and do without the lamp. Or use the light from your phone or from a small flashlight. Make a list of the things that enrich your life and a list of those that don't.

Clean Up!

Now, on to the next step! Before you can do some spring cleaning, you must organize your items. Create a library of what you own – yes, everything you own! Here is how to break it down:

- List of books, DVDs, CDs, video games, etc.
- Articles of clothing
- Furniture: beds, desks, drawers, cupboards, chairs etc.
- Décor: curtains, antiques, set-pieces, paintings, sculptures, etc.

Of course, your home will also consist of additional items such as appliances, but these are items which are replaced every now and then. For embracing the minimalist lifestyle, you need to focus on permanent items and realize what can go and what you must keep. Remember, this is not a competition; do not feel you need to let go of 50 items, or

75 items, or 100 items. Let go of what you feel is unnecessary. This will be a challenge, but do not worry. This lifestyle does not need to be embraced overnight; a gradual change is fine!

Books

Now that you have organized a list of all your books, it is time to filter out what is not needed. These are the questions to ask yourself:

- How long has it been since I read this book? Will I ever re-read it?
- Is this book obsolete? Do you still have an instruction manual for Microsoft Word 1998? Throw it away!
- Do I have a digital copy and/or audiobook of this book?
- Is this book in the public domain and therefore readily available for free access via the Internet?
- Is this book easily available at most libraries? Is it easily available for repurchasing at most bookstores?

If the answer to any of the last four questions is yes, then it is time to sell or give the book or books away. You will have noticed there are questions regarding if there is a digital copy available of your book. Throughout the book I will discuss moving to digital formats when appropriate. While the transition of digitizing all your materials is not an insistence, it is a recommendation as it is a surefire method to becoming minimalist. If you aim to replace your books, DVDs, and CDs with a digital format, you will have less clutter taking up space in your physical world.

Wardrobe

Often a hesitant glance at one's wardrobe is the deciding factor for many individuals to adopt a minimalist lifestyle. Apart from your personal library, your closet is what will need to be cleaned the most! Here is what you have to consider before giving away or selling your clothing:

- What clothing is absolutely necessary for your life? Do you work in a corporate setting and therefore need to own several suits? Do you need several uniforms? Do you need attire for a colder climate?
- What clothing does not fit you? You will be surprised how much of these items are hiding in your wardrobe!
- Do you have any clothing that exists solely for around the house? For sleeping? For messy days like repainting the house?
- And of course, don't forget about shoes!

If you are a corporate worker, perhaps it is best to hold on to the many suits. If not, see if you can limit it to two or three suits. Do you have any clothing items that serve a function which is not frequent? Maybe you have clothing suitable for outdoor work, but your lifestyle does not require much outdoor work. Let go of most outdoor work clothes then. Do you live in a tropical climate? Then there is certainly no need to have enough winter clothing to survive in Svalbard – the northernmost town on Earth!

A trick for adopting a minimalist wardrobe is to have a predetermined set of hangers. If you have 40 hangers, you should only own 40 items of clothing. If your clothing exceeds this number, let go of something. Another trick is when you re hang an article of clothing, twist the hanger to face toward you. Do this with every item of clothing you re-hang. After a while, check to see which hangers are not facing toward you. These are items that you do not wear often. See if these can be given away or sold.

Another rule which you may wish to follow is the "one in, one out" rule. If you purchase a new item of clothing, it should replace an existing item of clothing. If you purchase a new pair of jeans, see which existing pair you can bid farewell. Bought a new suit? It is time to say goodbye to the old suit!

When it comes to shoes, they should serve a function or they should make their way out of your wardrobe. Dress shoes serve a function, as they are necessary for formal occasions. You may need a pair of shoes for running, another for playing golf, and one for general athletics. But you do not need several pairs of each of these types of shoes. A pair or two pairs of flip-flops for the beach or around the house are sufficient.

Furniture And Décor

With furniture and décor, things get a bit tricky. Before looking at furniture, look at the function the furniture serves. If you have a bedside table, are essential items kept on top of it? Does the table have a built-in cabinet or drawers? Are they filled with essential items? How many essential items? If they are empty or nearly empty, you can downgrade to a simpler bedside table or discard the bedside table altogether and find another location for the items.

But what about furniture or décor that does not serve a function? Does your home look like an art gallery? Perhaps those paintings, trinkets, and sculptures should go. Do you have excess tables, chairs, or cabinets? Perhaps it is time to let them go. One of the goals of adopting the minimalist lifestyle is to make sure everything you own *serves a purpose or function.* Use that mindset when letting go of your possessions as well as when making a new purchase.

A clever trick in purchasing new furniture is to intentionally select something smaller, which has a lower capacity. For example, if your closet contains space for hanging clothes as well as a few drawers, see if the majority of your clothes can be hung up. Drawers should only be used for socks and underwear. If your clothing does not all fit in the hanging space, see what can be given away.

Similarly, if you buy a bedside table full of drawers, you may be tempted to fill them to the point of overflowing. If there is a lower capacity, it will force you to analyze and decide what can and should be given away.

Apart from being a lifestyle, you may be familiar with minimalism as an aesthetic. Minimalism is an artistic movement that has been carried over to home design. You do not need to embrace a particular aesthetic or any design guidelines when organizing your home or personal space but adopting the minimalist lifestyle will teach you how to organize your possessions in a manner which is aesthetically pleasing and practical.

Grab your notebook and pen and answer the following questions:

- Are there any spaces in your home which you feel need to be organized better? What do you want to change about these spaces?
- Is there a particular aesthetic you wish to follow?
- How often do you lose items due to the clutter? List the top 10 items which you have the difficulty finding – keys, wallet, important documents, etc.

Now, here are some guidelines to follow which will allow you to take a minimalist approach to designing your home and organizing your possessions:

- Have a tray to keep on-the-go items such as your keys, wallet, phone, etc.
- Have your on-the-go items in one section of your home; if possible, near the front door or an exit of the home. The idea is that when you need to grab these items, you do not need to roam around the home to collect them together
- Anything you wear should be kept in one place; accessories such as watches or jewelry should be in your closet along with your shoes and clothing.
- Keep related items in the same general area: For example, your DVD collection should not be too far from the television; all electronic accessories, such as chargers, batteries, wires, cords, etc. should be in one place.
- Organize a particular area for a specific purpose – so if you wanted to display all your family photos, find one space to keep your framed photographs and any family albums, etc. These photos are often scattered in various areas of the house, but for your own peace of mind, have them in a central location such as your living room.

- Have emergency and go-to items in a central location; these include first-aid kits, the iron and ironing board, cleaning supplies, tools, etc. It should be easy to access and easy to reach – unless there are small children in the house; adjust according to your situation.

- Aim to keep all silverware in one area of the kitchen as opposed to being distributed in different areas; same for plates, glasses, and coffee mugs. Also aim to eliminate repeated items; you do not need several knives, for instance. Keep all storage containers in one central area of the kitchen; keep condiments, spices, powders similarly in one central area. Napkins, paper towels, cloths, and all other cleaning supplies specifically for the kitchen should be kept in one area.

These are a few tricks and as you re-organize and redesign your home you will learn more efficient ways to have a minimalist home. The difficulty of finding your belongings by wading through your clutter will be gone. I strongly suggest you conduct an Internet search to see how fellow minimalists have designed their personal spaces, as you are sure to find inspiration on how to have a more functional home – as opposed to treating your home as a storage space!

Before we move on to the next chapter – here is a bit of homework!

- Organize and list all the items you own – excluding appliances.
- Determine if an item has a function or purpose; either write a short sentence or two highlighting the importance of the object or in checklist format, check off "yes" if an item has a purpose or function and "no" if it does not.
- Digitize what you can!
- Redesign and reorganize at least one room in your home.
- Start giving items away; see what you have not used in a while to determine what is not needed for your daily life.

Chapter Summary

- There are different styles of minimalism – find what works for you and what does not.
- Giving away your items is not as hard as it seems – you just need a game plan!
- Organize your personal space to determine your priorities with possessions.

In the next chapter, you will learn about the tricks of frugality.

Chapter Two: Frugality

In this chapter, you will learn about frugality, and how saving money is one of the key elements of minimalist living.

Frugality is an essential aspect of embracing the minimalist lifestyle. Before delving further, remember that frugality is not about being cheap or sacrificing what you desire. Adopting a sense of frugality is intended to help you save money without having to sacrifice what you would like to enjoy in life.

We live in a culture of instant gratification. This is the thing that makes it hardest for us to adopt a minimalist lifestyle. Instant gratification leads to consumerism, which is the antithesis of minimalism. Because you spent your paycheck immediately on a short-term pleasure, it now means months of slogging at work to save up for your dream vacation. As a result, the first rule of frugality is to set long-term goals.

Grab your notebook, turn to a blank page and jot down your answers to the following questions:

- What are your long-term purchasing goals? Do you wish to buy a house? A car?
- What are your short-term purchasing goals? Do you wish to buy a new suit? A DVD of a film you enjoy? Dinner at a popular restaurant?

Once you have written these goals down, you must determine how your short-term goals will hinder or postpone reaching your long-term goals.

Suppose you wish to take a three-day cruise to The Bahamas. The cost of the cruise is $600 per person. You are going with your significant other, so the cost of the cruise alone is $1200. Let us assume this is the exact amount you earn in a two-week work period. With the additional expenses of food, drinks, on-board amenities, and shopping on the islands, you have to put aside $2000 in total.

You also wish to treat your significant other to an expensive dinner at a newly-opened restaurant. This restaurant is managed by a celebrity chef, and as a result, the prices make your wallet tremble. If you spend $200 at the restaurant, how far will this put you back? Most likely, you can still attend the trip and cut back on souvenir shopping and fine dining. What about your need to purchase a new suit? If the suit costs $600 and you combine that with the dinner at the restaurant, you are now $800 short. You are now left with $1200 which is enough to take the cruise, but not enough to enjoy the amenities on board or in The Bahamas.

It would take you almost two weeks to earn back the amount needed for your original budget. This is the mindset to develop when it comes to frugality. Weigh the pros and cons of your short-term goals and see how they may hinder or postpone your long-term goals.

A popular phrase is "collect moments, not things," which is a way of saying that you should value experiences over material goods. This is a pivotal aspect of making the most out of the least. In the previous example on thinking in the long-term, you chose taking a holiday to The Bahamas over eating at a particular restaurant and purchasing a new suit.

We tend to value material things above all else, but we only value individual items for a short time. Do you value the Christmas present from last Christmas? What are your feelings toward your phone once the new model is released? Your budget should go toward experiences which cannot be done at any time, but that will help you create memories. You can purchase a phone at any time; you can eat at a restaurant at any time; most likely, you cannot go on vacation at any time.

Grab your notebook and turn to a blank page. Answer the following questions:

- What are the top five experiences which you would like to experience? A vacation? Skydiving?
- What are the top five material goods you wish to purchase? Are they replacing a previous model or are they in addition to what you own?
- Using what you have learned, determine how a material good will eliminate or postpone the opportunity for an experience. For example, if you purchase the new model of a smartphone, will it postpone your dream vacation?

We will revisit this exercise in Chapter Three.

Debt

Getting out of debt is crucial. At times, debt is inevitable due to emergencies. However, you should not be in debt due to paying for luxurious clothes, a perfectly-cooked steak, or a new smartphone. Building your credit score is important and necessary for many things, but it should not be relied upon for every transaction. Pay off your bill as soon as you can and when you can pay in full – do so!

Perhaps you know someone who utilizes debt every chance they get but who is not worried about their debt, and despite being in debt, their spending habits have not changed – immensely slowing down the process of paying off their debt. It is often while someone is in debt that they decide to espouse the minimalist lifestyle. They decide to spend less and start selling their possessions without prejudice in order to pay off their debt as quickly as possible.

While I want you to make the most out of life via minimalism, it may be necessary to sacrifice many pleasures at first to pay off all your debt. You may need to postpone that cruise to The Bahamas or that dinner at the new restaurant to pay off your debt. Trust me, once you are debt-free, it will be worth it, and you will have the *time* and *freedom* to pursue all of your desires.

Please note that none of this is financial advice. If you are in debt, it is best to consult with a professional financial advisor. But remember, the sooner you pay off your crippling debt, the better!

Digitizing

I have already briefly mentioned digitizing. While digitizing is optional and may or may not be to your liking, I want you to consider it as a method of adopting the minimalist lifestyle. As stated before, if you digitize your media, then your shelves will not overflow with printed books, DVDs, or CDs.

Think about what else you own which could use digitizing. After digitizing your items, you do not necessarily need to dispose of the items; if you don't, you will always have a backup. Please note that some documents, such as medical records, tax records, legal records, etc., may require a hard copy to be presented, so do not dispose of them even if they are digitized.

Grab your notebook and pen and answer the following:

- What important records do you own which could use digitizing?
- Do you have any printed photographs which could be digitized?
- What about any letters sent via snail mail back in the olden days?

Depending on how many of these documents and prints you own, digitizing them may be an extremely lengthy process. But do not worry, this does not need to be completed as soon as possible. Take time to scan and digitize your content and what does not need to be kept as a hard copy can be discarded. Digitizing is an excellent method for clearing up unnecessary clutter.

You Own Money, Money Does Not Own You

And do not let anyone tell you otherwise! We do inhabit a world where we need money to meet our basic needs. The minimalist lifestyle is not asking you to devalue your money; rather, it is asking you to not be controlled by your money. Just as the lifestyle is not against possessions, but rather against being owned by possessions, you must ensure that having, accumulating, and spending money is not be the central focus of your existence.

Take a moment to think about how you have chased money and how it has controlled your life. You might be surprised when you reflect upon the times when you put yourself into a financial pickle which could have been easily avoided.

Grab your notebook and pen and answer the following questions in as much detail as possible:

- How often do you make impulse and unnecessary purchases? On average, what is the amount of money you spend?
- How often have you cancelled a social occasion or important event to work extra in order to earn more money?
- Have you ever voluntarily worked on a day off, including a day off that you requested?
- Do you leap at the opportunity to fill in for a colleague to earn more money?
- How often have you aimed to have an increase in pay because you felt your current pay is insufficient?

- How often have you decided to work additional hours to earn money to purchase something you did not need?
- How often have you decided to take a side job or one-time gig to earn extra money?
- How long does it take you to earn your paycheck?
- On average, how quickly do you spend your paycheck?
- How often have you worked to earn extra money because you were bored and felt there was nothing else for you to do with your time?

I realize this is an exhausting list of questions – but that is exactly how I expect you to feel: exhausted! If many or all of these questions are applicable to you, it means that you have exhausted yourself time and time again in the pursuit of money. This may be inevitable and necessary due to your personal situation – but if the majority of your pursuit of money is because of any of the reasons above, then perhaps it is time to embrace the minimalist approach to money.

Shopping

After all this instruction on frugality, it may seem paradoxical to discuss shopping. But rest assured, shopping is a necessity and the minimalist lifestyle is not asking you to forgo it. Luxury and name brands are also not enemies of the minimalist lifestyle. It is just that the minimalist lifestyle is not married to such brands in the manner that consumerism is. If you need to purchase a new laptop, it is not anti-minimalist to go for the latest model by Apple or Microsoft; you do not need to buy a cheap $200 generic model with limited features. Purchase the laptop that will suit your needs and is reliable. This is a possession you should value – as a minimalist should value each of his or her possessions. If you were to purchase a pair of sunglasses, it is perfectly acceptable to purchase them from a luxury brand instead of opting for a cheap pair from your local convenience store. You should value these sunglasses – they should not end up on an endless pile of sunglasses. If buying the luxury glasses makes you value them more, then it's perfectly fine.

Chapter Summary

- Frugality is the name of the game when it comes to minimalism.
- Be aware of how you spend.
- When you do have to shop, make measured decisions on what you purchase.

In the next chapter you will learn about arranging your environment to suit your minimalist lifestyle.

Chapter Three: Environment

In this chapter, you will learn how to create an environment conducive for minimalism and how minimalism can be conducive to the environment!

Now that you have given away your items and determined value for what you have kept, it is time to organize your possessions. For minimalists, placing and decorating your personal space is of the utmost importance. Have a look at the different areas of your home. Could they be organized better? Since you are becoming a minimalist, these areas *have* to be organized better!

The Office

Whether you occasionally visit your desk or are glued to it for the majority of your day, your desk must be organized well. If your desk has drawers, open them and inspect the items. If the drawers are cluttered by anything unnecessary, see what can be discarded or given away. The drawers should only contain essential items needed for the work you conduct on your desk. Stationery should be plentiful in the drawers. If you keep a computer on your desk, maybe an extra charger or mouse can be kept in the drawers.

On the desk itself, keep what needs to be used to complete your work. This may include your computer, a legal pad, immediate stationery such as pens, sticky pads, and a stapler. Additional items may include a lamp. Avoid adorning your desk with unnecessary decorations such as photographs. They may seem like a staple on any work desk, but remember, you are a minimalist! This is not to say these unnecessary items should be forbidden on the desk, but they are to be used sparingly. The items on your desk should serve a function or at the very least should add value. At no point should you look at your desk and feel that it is cluttered.

The Bathroom

The bathroom is usually a place for clutter. Observe your bathroom now and see what could be removed. Here are some best practices for a minimalist bathroom:

- Keep one toothbrush, one tube of toothpaste, and one bottle of mouthwash at a time.

- If you shave often, purchase blades in bulk. If not, only keep a small case of blades. You might even switch to an electronic razor. *You will find a great way to save money on razor blades in Chapter Four.*

- Look at any cosmetics that are kept in the bathroom. If any of them are *not* used on a regular basis, throw them away.

- Limit the amount of bathing towels and hand towels that are kept in the bathroom. Keep one for each member of the household and no more than two extra per member.

- And of course, the bathroom does not need to be adorned or cluttered with unnecessary decorations.

The Bedroom

Our bedrooms are often multi-purpose. If you are able to separate your bedroom from your home office, you should aim to do so. If not, ensure that your workspace does not overwhelm your bedroom. For a minimalist bedroom, your bed should be the main focus of the room. The room should not have any additional clutter if it can be helped.

Bedrooms often are laden with décor, but as a minimalist, you should aim to only have décor that serves a function or truly adds to the room. A painting that reflects your personality works; a few framed photographs are also a great addition.

Clutter

Often when we move into a new home, we look at an empty space and think, *what can I do with this space?* We may even boast about how much we have budgeted for material goods that will fill up this space. But you are a minimalist – if you see an empty space, do not think of filling it unless it has a function. It is okay to find an empty space to place a spare bed, a desk, or your luggage. But there is no need to fill this empty space with material goods which you will not value after some time or use on a frequent basis.

Sometimes the greatest obstacle in removing clutter is the sentimental value that a material good may possess. This may be the reason why we are such hoarders! As I have discussed, consumerism has caused us to purchase material goods that provide us with temporary satisfaction. Some material goods have sentimental value for us and we feel a sense of emptiness without them.

Remember, there is no requirement to give anything away; just evaluate the value or function it adds to your life. Here are things to consider when evaluating your sentimental items:

- Can this item add value to someone else's life? Maybe you value an item of clothing from a loved one. However, someone less fortunate may need or greatly benefit from this item of clothing.

- Can this item be digitized? As mentioned previously, sentimental photographs or letters can be digitized. Items such as diaries can also be digitized.

- Is this item a burden to maintain? Perhaps you have a piece of furniture or an antique which has been in the family for several decades. However, hanging onto it causes more grief than joy. Consider selling it.

- Can this item be given to another loved one? Maybe you do not have to discard a sentimental good – perhaps you can pass it on to a fellow family member.

When creating your environment, you want to live deliberately. The items you keep or purchase should serve some necessary purpose in your life. In removing the clutter from your personal space, see what is unnecessary and can be given away. Another viewpoint is, *does this item have a simpler alternative?* Do you have a clock on your wall? As there are an infinite amount of ways you can check the time digitally, does that wall really need a clock on it? This rule can particularly be applied with furniture and décor. Aim to eliminate items that do not have a purpose or replace them with a simpler alternative.

Did you ever lose anything as a child? I am sure you lost a toy and it caused you immense grief upon losing it. But after some time, you move on, and you do not miss it. You perhaps did not realize it, but you came to a realization that the toy is not essential and does not add value to your life. I am certain you also played hide-and-seek and recall the rules. So, here is a new exercise involving objects and hiding:

- Take an item which you are unsure of – you may feel it has no value, but you hesitate to give it away.
- Hide the item. Obviously, you will remember where it is, but keep it in a place which is not easily accessible. For example, if you are unsure if you need the $300 fountain pen, keep it in a safe or on a high shelf – anywhere that is not easily reachable while you are seated at your desk.
- If after a week you are not tempted to use the item and you do not attempt to recover the item, it is time for you to part ways.

As you have been reading this book, I am sure you have shuddered a few times at the thought of giving away your prized possessions. Many individuals will advocate for giving away without thinking. As you have hoarded items, these individuals insist you give away most of your items in hordes! While there is nothing wrong with this method, I am going to advocate taking the slow and steady path to decluttering.

Grab your notebook and pen and jot this down:

- Make a note of the specific areas of your home which have the most clutter – for example, you can state that your wardrobe is overburdened with your clothes. Your bedside table is also overflowing. As is the small cupboard by the front door.

- Take a cursory glance at each of these areas and choose at least one item which you would like to give away immediately. You can choose as many as you feel necessary but ensure that there is at least one item.

- Set a deadline of no more than a week away for when you will give away each item. For example, "I will give away my brown dress shirt a week from today," and "I will give away the unused baseball bat three days from now."

- Follow through! If you are going to a charity shop, secondhand shop, or friend's place – organize time during your day to give away the item. If you decide you will give your baseball bat to a nearby school for their baseball team, ensure that you arrange an appointment at the school on the day you wrote you would give away the baseball bat.

This practice should be introductory. Eventually it should provide you with a sense of discipline and make it easier to give away what you no longer need.

And before we move on, here are some quick tricks to speed up your decluttering process in regard to stationery:

- Count how many pens and pencils are in the house and throw away any excessive amount. You decide what qualifies as excessive, but five per person in the household should be sufficient.
- If there are any other writing utensils, such as markers, only keep what you regularly use. If you only use a black permanent marker, then the other colors should be departing your home.
- You only need one stapler, one pair of scissors, a single hole puncher, and one tape holder.

Zero Waste

This is an aspect of minimalism which is seldom discussed, but I expect will rapidly garner traction. A benefit of decluttering and ensuring that clutter does not enter your environment again leads to setting a goal of Zero Waste. Depending on your location and lifestyle, Zero Waste may not be achievable, but see what you can do. It is one of the most environmentally conscious aspects of the minimalist lifestyle and will benefit the environment as well as your personal life – not to mention your bank account.

Here are a few tasks to get you started:

- Once again, digitize all paperwork and then discard. Do not discard important documents such as medical records or legal files, as a hard copy may always be needed – do your research on this one.
- Aim to have as few plastic bags in the house as possible.
- Find alternatives to buying water in plastic bottles. Also have alternatives for storing such liquids in your home. If you go to a coffee shop, see if they can pour your coffee in a thermal bottle you carry. Not all shops will allow their employees to do this, so be understanding; however, being eco-friendly is a growing trend and more stores are sure to catch on!
- Shop with your own cloth bags. Again, see if your purchased products can be kept in your own cloth bags. Not all shops will allow this, so once again be patient and understanding with them.
- Respectfully decline a free non-disposable gift you may receive at a university campus, festival, fair, etc. This is probably one of the biggest contributors to the clutter in our homes.

- If you need information from a flyer, instead of taking a printed copy of the flyer, take a picture of the flyer, or note the details on your phone.
- Send materials digitally; avoid printing out anything when you can!

Travel

One of the largest subgroups of the minimalist community is travelers. Whether you live life as a nomad or travel once in a while, there is a minimalist approach to travel which can benefit you greatly. Have you often traveled to a place and by the look of your luggage, it would appear as if you were relocating to the place? The minimalist approach will teach you to be compact and precise in your packing, even if you actually are relocating.

Here are some great tips:

- Opt for smaller electronics. Attempt to carry a tablet as opposed to a laptop. If a laptop is crucial, see if it is feasible to trade-in your current model for a smaller, lighter, and more compact model.
- Roll your clothing as opposed to folding; this should take up less space in your bag.
- Why not try a minimalist wallet? We are told to "fatten our wallets," but a minimalist wallet will

carry the necessary cards, licenses, and amount of cash that you need.

- For longer trips, you may want to forgo the toiletries and purchase them once you arrive at your destination.
- Unless you really need to, do not get sucked into the duty-free shopping at the airport!

Chapter Summary

- You can design your personal space to tie in with your minimalist lifestyle.
- You can be particularly conscious and adopt a Zero Waste lifestyle.
- There are ways which you can apply minimalism to your travel plans.

In the next chapter, you will learn how to be more deliberate when you spend your money.

Chapter Four: Deliberate Spending

In this chapter, you will learn how to spend with awareness and how to value your possessions.

We have discussed at length how to give away items that you no longer need. Yet I have also stressed that minimalism is not against purchasing items. The idea is not to keep you from shopping, but to help you become more *deliberate* with your shopping habits.

Take these factors into consideration before embarking on your next shopping spree:

- Are you purchasing items which have a function? Are you purchasing a new kettle or coffee maker? A rice cooker? A portable GPS system for when you travel? A new pair of running shoes for your upcoming marathon? A new laptop since your current one has become tired and weary? Or are you adding clothes to your closet that you do not need? If you already have a great pair of running shoes, do you need another?

- Is there more than enough space in your home? Have you ever purchased groceries and had difficulty placing them in the refrigerator? Your possessions should be able to easily fit; if they don't, then perhaps you should free up some space before purchasing anything new.
- How long will you keep this item? Are you buying a Christmas present for yourself which will be replaced or discarded the following Christmas?

If you ever make a list of what you wish to purchase before going shopping, take the above factors into consideration. Your shopping list is sure to decrease, and your purchases will become more *deliberate*.

The above method also works in budgeting. The minimalist lifestyle approach to budgeting should teach you to take several factors in deciding how much of your budget should be allocated toward different purchases. One thing that the minimalist lifestyle – and this book – advocates is living your best life. I want minimalism to help you live a better life than you are living now; the quality of your life should improve due to minimalism.

The main aspect of improving one's quality of life is freedom. We equate the amount of our finances with our personal freedom. But if our money is continuously spent, do we really have freedom? Managing your finances as a minimalist will compel you to analyze each purchase and make measured decisions for future purchases.

Regretful Spending

Take a pause. I want you to reflect on a time when you made a purchase and later regretted it. You regretted it because you realize that had you forgone this purchase, you could have made a better purchase or saved your money for something better. Remember the example of spending $200 on an expensive dinner when that money could go toward a once-in-a-lifetime cruise to The Bahamas?

Grab your notebook and pen and answer the following:

- What was a purchase I made which I later regretted?
- Why did I regret it? Was it a waste of money? Could I have gotten a better deal? Could the money have gone toward something better? Have I gotten into debt due to a frivolous purchase?

Write a few sentences answering these two questions and then take a moment to reflect before reading further.

Now that you've reflected on it, I am sure that you are kicking yourself due to a regretful purchase. This is going to stop once you begin to take measured decisions. You may have heard of "If...then" statements in computing; well, I am going to have you apply this statement when making decisions while shopping.

Here is a possible scenario: You are on your lunch break at work. After you finish your meal, you opt for dessert. Having dessert is not necessary, and your hunger has already been satisfied from your meal. The dessert costs $8, which is a disposable amount for you. As a result, you do not think much about spending the $8. The amount may be small, and you may not be losing an opportunity to purchase something else. But supposing you spend $8 each day that you work and assuming it is five days per week, you have spent $40 over the course of one week. Again, this may not seem like a large amount of money. It may seem that by spending this $40 you are not sacrificing anything. But all of a sudden, your favorite musician is performing a concert in your area and the cost is $40. At the time tickets are being sold, you are in a bit of a financial pickle and you are unable to spend $40. It is at such time when you realize ordering those desserts has prevented you from purchasing the concert tickets. So, *if* you spend $40 over a week on dessert, *then* you will not be able to attend the concert.

This is a small example, but this mentality should be carried over when making bigger decisions. Say you are planning on purchasing a car and you are required to pay $300 per month over a course of a few years. If you are unable to make the minimum payment, an interest charge is placed on the $300. Of course, when possible, you can pay over the minimum payment and pay off the car sooner. By making this goal and committing to it, you will take measured decisions about your purchases. You will not recklessly spend. So, *if* you avoid reckless and unnecessary purchases, *then* you will be able to pay off your car on time or earlier!

The minimalist approach should train you to not make impulse purchases and make sound financial decisions in advance. You will recall I wrote about assessing your short-term purchase goals and comparing them with your long-term purchase goals. I want you to return to this exercise but apply the "If…then" thought process to your goals.

Grab your notebook and pen and write down three short-term purchase goals and three-long term purchase goals. See how the short-term goals may affect the long-term goals.

Here are some examples:

- If I purchase a new flat screen television, then it will take me an extra six months to pay off my car.
- If I regularly by a cup of coffee each day before work, then I am spending $25 a week. This is

$100 a month which I can use toward booking a short stay in a hotel in six months' time!

- If I allocate $1000 toward shopping for Christmas presents, then I may not have $1000 allocated for my tuition which I will owe in three months.

Practice this for planning your financial goals and purchases. You should eventually get into this mentality every time you make a purchase; this is how a minimalist makes sound financial decisions.

Food

Don't worry, I'm not asking you to go on a diet! Many minimalists do embrace particular diets, but I will not ask you to not to ever indulge yourself, go on a fashionable diet, or cut any food out of your diet. Those avenues are available and may cause much simplicity to your life, but I will look at managing your food habits from a financial standpoint.

Returning to the example of spending $40 a week on dessert, take a moment to reflect upon how much money you spend on extra or excessive food. Do not include the groceries you need to purchase for now – I will expand upon this later. First focus on how often you eat at restaurants and how much you order. Whether you already do this or not, henceforth keep your receipts from ordering takeout and food shopping and keep them safely as a reference. You will need to refer to these receipts for the following exercises.

Let us start with recording eating out and restaurant expenses. Grab your notebook and pen and do the following:

- Record the amount of money you spent at restaurants or eating out in the previous month; if you have more time, I would suggest recording as many months as you can go back and calculate the total and the average amount of money spent over the duration you chose.
- Look at your receipts in detail – observe how many times you ordered an appetizer and dessert just for yourself. Calculate the total amount as well as the average amount of money spent on appetizers and desserts. You can separate these two categories or bundle them together.
- Record any time you ordered a drink which was not free; so basically, any time you did not order water! Calculate the total amount as well as the average amount of money spent on these drinks; Ignore times when you ordered a large pitcher of beer for the table – focus on drinks that were just for you.

Now that you have these amounts recorded, I want you to mull over where else this money could be allocated. Let us presume you spent a total of $700 at restaurants over a month with $300 on appetizers, desserts, and drinks. With $300 you can make a monthly payment toward a car – as the example I gave before outlines. It can be used for additional adventures on your next holiday. It can be used for university textbooks or paying for an undergraduate-level class. Or you can simply save it and get into the habit of saving $300 a month for $3600 saved per year.

So, while I am not saying you should never order appetizers, desserts, or drinks, each time you eat out think about whether or not you need these additions. If your main course satisfies your hunger, is there a need for appetizers or desserts? And stick to water as often as you can with your food – your bank account will thank you later! Remember the "If...then" practice with any type of purchase; ordering takeout and going to restaurants should all be tackled with the minimalist approach.

Now let us move on to the second part of spending money on food: grocery shopping. Once again, keep the receipts from when you purchase groceries to record in your notebook.

In your notebook, record the following:

- How much money you spent purchasing groceries over a particular duration – remember the longer the duration, the better.

- Detail how much is spent on particular groups of items: how much is spent on fruits and vegetables, meats, drinks, snacks, desserts, etc. Discount one-time purchases such as the time you splurged on a birthday cake last month. Focus on your regular purchases.
- Record how often these groceries are consumed: are your fruits and vegetables consumed regularly? Does your pasta sit in the pantry for months before you cook it? Are there cans of soup which have passed their expiration date and you did not even attempt to eat?

Grocery shopping is a necessity, but you are probably overspending on your grocery shopping. Once again, we will use the minimalist approach to minimize our spending and therefore maximize our quality of life.

Turn to a blank page in your notebook and jot down the answers to these questions:

- What items on your grocery list are unessential? What do you only have once in a blue moon?
- What items on your grocery list seem to never get consumed?
- What items on your grocery list take the longest to consume?

Perhaps you buy a tub of ice cream and only have it as an occasional treat. This is an example of an unessential item. Maybe you buy soda or another high-caffeine drink in preparation for a busy day of work. Cut down or eliminate these items to save your money.

What does not seem to be consumed? If it is those cans of soup, then they should be eliminated from your shopping list. If there are items which take a while to consume, then they should also be eliminated from your shopping list.

Here is an exercise: on your next grocery shopping trip, shop for only your essential items. Eliminate *all* unnecessary purchases. Compare the total cost of your bill with your previous bill, or a bill that contains many unessential items. Look at how much money you saved and write down at least three things the money could be used for. It could be as simple as paying a bill quicker, treating yourself to going to the cinema, or simply as a saving toward a long-term goal. Once again, this analysis of your purchases will show you how minimizing your purchases will maximize your quality of life and bring greater returns and rewards.

Don't Discount That!

Discounts are a minimalist's best friend. As you have read, a prominent aspect of the minimalist budget is saving money and spending less money. There is no objection to spending money and money will have to be spent. So why not save money when you do have to spend it? Here are some simple tips to save money while shopping:

- Always look for coupons. You may find coupons for a variety of shops on the Internet, through apps, or even in your mailbox.

- If possible, hold off on a purchase until there are sales. During a particular season or day there may be significant discounts on goods which otherwise would not be there.

- Look at various options for purchasing an item. You may walk into a bookshop and see a book you like being sold for $20. On the Internet, a quick search can find several online stores which may sell the same book for a lower price. If you are fine with purchasing a secondhand edition, again look online as you may find a cheaper option.

- Do not splurge on one-time purchases if possible. Let us assume you live in a climate which is warm all year round. However, for every winter holiday you visit your family who live in a much colder climate where it snows. For this short trip, you will need a few cold-weather clothes. After this trip, the clothes will not be worn again until the following winter trip. You should not be spending lots of money on these clothes. Remember, they are not used often and if by chance you grow out of them, you will have to spend money again. Find the lowest price you can, without compromising on the quality. Similarly, if you live in a cold climate and visit a beach resort on a warm tropical island once a year, there is no need to own several swimsuits!

- Borrow or rent if you can help it. If you are attending one wedding in a year, and are required to wear a tuxedo or formal dress for the occasion, would you purchase the tuxedo or formal dress? It is better to borrow or rent the outfit for the wedding and return it afterward.

- Use rewards toward purchases. Perhaps you have a credit card which gives you points after making purchases. Those points can be used toward purchases to receive a discount. Some credit cards may even offer points in the form of cash; if so, you may even be able to transfer the cash to your bank account!

- Another way to receive a discount which also ties into frugality: if you receive a gift card, make sure you use it! If possible, do not purchase items which will exceed the amount on the gift card or ensure that the gift card will cover over half the total cost of the items.

Here is one thing to keep in mind: a minimalist is also an expert researcher. You must be relentless in your search for the best products with the best prices. Remember, the lowest price should not equal the lowest quality. Similarly, if the price is high the quality of the product should be on par. If you are purchasing a tangible good, ensure that it will last a long time. A one-time expensive purchase on a long-lasting good is cheaper than having to repurchase the good at a lower price on a frequent basis.

For example, research alternate solutions for purchasing goods at a lesser cost. I have provided the example of purchasing from a bookshop versus purchasing online, but it does not stop there. Just as I have instructed you to be relentless in analyzing your purchases and thinking about the trade-offs, I would like you to be relentless in your research. Always see what alternative solutions are available. Here are some examples which you may want to adopt right away:

- For shaving: Razor blades can be pricy. Look into subscription services available for both men and women which are lower in cost and send you razor blades on a monthly basis or as needed.
- For clothing: There are endless options – there are always thrift shops and charity shops to purchase secondhand clothing. Look at outlet shops to purchase name-brand clothing at discounted costs. If possible, only do your clothing shopping during seasons where sales are prominent. And of course, there are

numerous subscription services which send you brand new designer clothing on a monthly basis or as needed.

- For transportation: When driving your car is not needed, explore alternative routes such as public transportation. If walking or bicycling are available options – take them! Also, as a minimalist, your focus should be on reliability, comfort, and safety, not the visual appeal or status that a car would bring you.

- When you can, do-it-yourself. More on this below:

Do You DIY?

We have become accustomed to having the simplest of tasks done by others. If we do not have time to clean the clutter in our house, we hire a housekeeper. We may even hire a cook or only eat at restaurants or order food to be delivered. If something in the house needs maintenance, we have a plethora of individuals to call. When we need to clean our cars, we find someone else or go to a drive-through car wash and let the machines do the hard work! But as a minimalist, take every opportunity to do-it-yourself.

First, think about washing your car. If you do not do this already, calculate how much money you spend in a year on having your car washed. Depending on how often you do this, the amount can vary greatly. Nevertheless, use the principles you have learned to calculate what you could do with the money saved. I am sure whatever the amount, you have better things to do with the saved money.

Cleaning one's home is at the top of any "most loathsome chores" list. Perhaps one of the biggest reasons is due to the fact that cleaning our homes is a lengthy and arduous task. However, minimalists often do not find stress in cleaning after decluttering. When you have decluttered your home, start cleaning it; you might be surprised to find that you do not find it as stressful as before. Not to mention, you will be saving money and being frugal – which is what minimalism is all about!

Here are some other activities which you can aim to do yourself. They may or may not work for you, but see which ones you can attempt:

- Cutting/styling your own hair. See if you can forgo a visit to the barber or hairstylist.
- Repairing appliances.
- Additional construction needed around the house as well as home improvement and repair.
- Sewing – either for repairing clothing or making your own!
- Become a computer expert so you do not have to take your computer to the store if/when an issue arises; this skill can carry on to any

hardware-related issue such as fixing a cracked screen on your phone.

- Learn a skill like programming so you can build a software for your needs and not need to purchase an existing software.

- Learn a skill which you outsource to others relating to your professional life. For example, if you need a website built to show your qualifications and portfolio, it is time-saving and money-saving to build it yourself rather than to hire a professional web designer.

- Learn how to file your own taxes. For your own peace of mind, you may prefer to always use an expert such as a Certified Public Accountant, but there is no harm in learning the procedure yourself.

- Polish and repair your shoes.

- If your home needs to be re-painted, grab a bucket, brushes, and some overalls! You will save money and bring out your inner Picasso!

- Build your own home gym or basic workout equipment and forgo the gym membership.

See what you can do to minimize your spending and maximize your time. A challenge you can give yourself is to write the above list – along with any other set of do-it-yourself skills you deem worthy – in your notebook and cross off any skill you have mastered. Think of it as a bucket list.

Think Like The Rich

Interestingly enough, some of the world's greatest minimalists are its richest inhabitants. Many millionaires and billionaires adopt minimalist lifestyles to help save money and cultivate frugal habits. Here are a few which may work for you:

Warren Buffett always comes to mind when thinking of frugal billionaires. The main point of interest here is that one of the richest men in the world has forgone living in a penthouse of a skyscraper and continues to live in the same modest house he purchased in 1958. Make sure the roof over your head fits. If you are a family of four, a house is perhaps a necessity, but maybe a mansion is not. If you are a single person or a couple, a small one-bedroom apartment should be all you need.

I wrote before about opting for public transportation when you can. Ingvar Kamprad, the founder of IKEA, was known to take public transportation despite being a billionaire and one of Europe's richest men. If you live in an area that offers excellent public transportation, take advantage of it when possible. Better still, if you live in an area where you can easily walk or ride a bicycle to a location, do so! Avoiding driving your car saves money on gas, and if your area does not require you to own a car, then you are saving thousands by not owning one!

Steve Jobs was a great minimalist where his wardrobe was concerned, and Mark Zuckerberg carries on this tradition. Both entrepreneurs stuck to a simple uniform which simplified their life decisions and displayed their frugality. You do not need to commit to a uniform as such, but these examples show you how to not give an overwhelming importance to purchasing a variety of clothing from luxury and expensive brands.

Many individuals who are now rich owe in part their financial success to frugality and minimalism. Their relationships with frugality and minimalism have not dwindled, which is what factors into their continued financial success. Adopt these habits – learn from the best!

Chapter Summary

- Make deliberate choices about how you spend your money. Do you need that coffee every morning? Could you use that money for something else?
- DIY to stretch your budget.
- Many of the richest people in the world have adopted minimalist values. Take lessons from the best!

In the next chapter, you will learn that minimalism goes beyond the physical world; that time is of the essence; and that work does not necessarily have to be the main focus of your life.

Chapter Five: Reclaim Your Time

In this chapter, you will learn how to reclaim your time with a minimalist mindset.

It is time for a bit of work! So far, you have learned how to declutter your belongings, organize your space, manage your finances, and make deliberate purchases. Before learning about the next topics, I would like you to take a pause and develop your minimalist plan.

The Minimalist Plan

Grab your notebook and pen and answer the following questions. They may seem esoteric, but this will prepare you to commit to the minimalist lifestyle and train your mind to adapt to the minimalist mindset. A few sentences per question is sufficient.

- Why do you want to become minimalist?
- What are some bad habits you possess which you feel can be eradicated by the minimalist lifestyle?
- What progress have I made so far and what still needs to improve?

A second part to your minimalist Plan should be a Progress Log. You will use this to track your progress so far. Once you have answered the third question from above, you will have a clear idea of how to design your Progress Log.

Begin each page of your Progress Log as follows:

- Write the date at the top.
- Write a few sentences on your mood; are you feeling relaxed, stressed, or neutral? How has minimalism affected you to this date?
- Have you given away anything?
- Have you purchased anything?
- What have you reduced? Shopping habits, time spent doing unproductive things, etc.
- What has increased or improved? Do you have more free time? Have you saved money for more enjoyable experiences?

How often you record your Progress Log is up to you, but I would recommend doing it once a week, either at the beginning or at the end of the week. If you find changes are gradual, perhaps increase the frequency to bi-monthly or even once a month. The Progress Log is a great way to see how minimalism is improving your life, and what still needs working on.

Go Digital!

I have mentioned digitizing your printed materials as an excellent method to declutter. However, it is vital to know that decluttering does not only apply to the physical world. While we are moving toward digitizing our files and our important records, we must ensure that our digital space does not get cluttered as well. As we spend more and more of our lives on our computers and on the Internet, the eventual clutter will affect our well-being just as the clutter in the physical world does. Remember, you are a minimalist and the quality of your digital life is as important as your quality of life in the physical world.

Here are the steps to cleaning your hard drive and your cloud:

- Unsubscribe to mailing lists and newsletters. Every time we make an account on a website, we intentionally or unintentionally subscribe to their mailing list. There may be many newsletters we gladly subscribed to because we felt the information would benefit us or entertain us. But how many newsletters do you religiously read? Many of them are cluttering your inbox. Take some time out of your day and unsubscribe to them.

- Delete unnecessary documents and images. Did you ever save an interesting article you read on the web? Or download a meme you found funny once? Your computer is probably overburdened with these materials and if they are not something you view on a regular basis, they should go.

- Delete unused applications. Uninstall them and trash them.

- Delete unnecessary emails. This ties in to unsubscribing to mailing lists and newsletters. After you have prevented more emails coming your way, go through your inbox and delete any emails you have which you do not need to refer back to.

Of course, our digital space does not stop at our computers. Our digital experience extends to the portable device in our pockets. We are addicted to our phones and we can simplify and get more out of life if we apply the minimalist approach to our phones, as well.

Here are some steps to having a minimalist phone:

- Use your phone for its original purpose: communication. I presume you own a smartphone, which means that your phone is not simply used to make calls or write text messages. You watch entire films, check your social media accounts, take photographs, play games, and invest in the stock market. These may come as a convenience and there is no requirement to remove every app; but look through the apps you have not used in a month and delete them.

- Look at apps you do use and determine the necessity of using them. Checking your credit card and bank statements via your phone are extremely convenient. But if there is no need to continuously check them, delete the corresponding apps. Do you need to watch an entire film on your phone? Only if you are not a fan of the selection on an airplane. And unless social media management is your career and you need to constantly be on a platform, delete those apps from your phone.

- Routinely save your images and videos to your computer or to a cloud or to both. Then, delete them permanently from your phone. Do the same for music, podcasts, audiobooks, and e-books.

- Remove your email accounts from your phone. Again, if it is crucial for you to check your email for work or academic purposes or if you are always needed, then you will have to keep it. Otherwise, delete the accounts.

- Turn off notifications. Unless it is an emergency or necessary for work purposes, do you need to be notified of every message, every Facebook post, every Instagram like?
- Turn off your phone altogether, silence it, or turn off your cellular data. How often have you gone out to dinner with a friend and spent more time interacting on your phone than with your friend? It may not be practical, and you may need to be on standby, but if you can, try one of the three options so that you do not get distracted by your phone.

And let us not forget decluttering our Internet space! Does your Netflix queue or YouTube "Watch Later" list seem endless? Is your RSS reader filled with hundreds of feeds you cannot recall subscribing to? If you scroll through your bookmarks, you probably will not be able to describe the content of each website among them. Our Internet space is also cluttered and could use a minimalist makeover.

Let us begin with your media watching queue – whether on Netflix, Hulu, YouTube, or any of the hundred video-streaming websites. I am almost certain you have an endless number of videos in your queues which you will "eventually" get to watch. Take time out of your day and REMOVE videos which you know you will not get through.

With a sense of apprehension, I would look through my Netflix and Hulu queues and see a list of films which I did not recall adding to the queue. I would see the short descriptions of the films and rack my brain trying to remember what about the film's synopsis I found appealing. If I did not have a strong desire to see the film, it would be removed from the queue. If the film was well-known and I could see it at any time either via a streaming service or by finding a DVD at the local library, it would be removed from the queue.

The same mindset should be applied to "Watch Later" on YouTube and other similar websites. Perhaps you need to take time to watch the long documentary, or an informative video. But does the latest cat video need to be in your queue? And if you subscribe to a channel, you can visit the channel's page at any time to watch its videos – there is no need to keep them in your "Watch Later" list. With subscriptions, do a clean-up every now and then. You will be surprised at how many YouTube channels you have subscribed to on impulse. Maybe you liked one video and you felt that subscribing to the channel was the obvious next step. You may have subscribed to a channel based on an interest or need which you no longer have! Clean up!

Digital Social Life

And of course, let us not forget about social media. Social media takes up much of our life and with or without realizing us it, it adds complexity to our life. As minimalism is improving the quality of life through the means of simplicity, it is crucial that we use the minimalist approach on our various social media platforms.

Let's start with Facebook. How many friends do you have in your life? Over a thousand? I highly doubt it, but I am sure that you have a gargantuan number of friends on Facebook. You may not realize it, but you are preventing yourself from living your best life because of this.

First of all, take a cursory glance at your Facebook feed. By any chance are there constant negative posts by your Facebook friends? I hope not, but it is very likely. If you are constantly seeing negative messages and they are consistently posted by the same individuals, then it may just be time to unfriend them from Facebook. By absorbing constant negativity, you are adding to the complexity of life – which you know by now is the antithesis to minimalism. You should take this same approach by quitting unnecessary Facebook groups as well as unfollowing Facebook pages which no longer serve your interests and just add to the endless noise. Facebook can be used for many things, but essentially it is a method to keep in touch with your friends and family. If possible, limit its usage to just this.

Just as I suggested using your smartphone for simply calling and texting, use Facebook for its original purpose as much as possible. Spend time communicating with friends and family, not watching mindless videos. I have discussed the importance of *freedom* in improving one's quality of life; when much of your time is wasted on social media, you are trading away your freedom to engage in more pleasurable activities which bring a greater value to your life.

I recommend applying this same attitude to all social media platforms. Look through the people you follow on Twitter and stop following ones who add no value or add harm to your life due to their negativity. On Instagram, are you following talented photographers whose photographs enrich your life by their beauty, or are you following users whose albums consist of endless selfies?

Even a professional networking website like LinkedIn comes with excess baggage. In an effort to network and make connections, we tend to accept invitations from anyone who has mutual connections. Even if they do not, we may add them because we feel it may benefit us in our professional lives. Before we know it, LinkedIn has become like Facebook! We are bombarded with unnecessary messages, we are asked to congratulate a connection on their new job – only to wonder, *who is this person again?* We have become servants to our careers, and therefore servants to *possible* connections who *may* be a great addition to our network. There is no need to connect with anyone and everyone on LinkedIn; connect with those you meet or collaborate with in your professional life.

Whether you are a professional marketer or not, we have all become entrapped in the numbers game on social media. How many followers, connections, likes, thumbs up, etc.

we have seems to matter a great deal to us. Depending on your situation, it may be necessary to grow an audience via social media to spread our message or our content for the sake of our careers, but we must not let the numbers own us. Numbers in the realm of social media have the same capacity as material goods in the physical world. So much so, that we will use our hard-earned money to purchase additional followers; we will go to extents such as following spam accounts which promise to grant us with hundreds of followers. This is the mentality which leads us to consider a real-world acquaintance worthy enough to become a Facebook friend; or feeling a fellow-suited professional at a career fair was more than welcome to join your LinkedIn network. The minimalist approach should teach you to only aim for more connections if it is necessary, and even still, one should not be owned by the numbers.

Digital Consumerism

Just as consumerism is an issue within the physical world, so is the issue prevalent in the digital world. Many of your purchases may occur in the digital world, and it may be cyberspace which is costing you your freedom.

Take a moment to analyze if any of these digital purchases are relevant to you:

- Music – do you purchase songs individually or buy entire albums from a service like iTunes?

- Movies – do you purchase movies and have a digital copy stored?
- E-books and audiobooks
- Apps and software
- Games

Any of these above purchases may increase the numbers on your bill and perhaps your debt. So, let us see how we can take the minimalist approach on these digital purchases. I am going to apply the "If…then" principle, but this time *then* will pose an alternate solution:

- If you regularly purchase music digitally, then you should consider subscribing to a music streaming service where you pay a monthly fee and have access to millions of songs which you can stream limitlessly. There are many services which allow you to stream these songs for free, under the condition that you hear a short advertisement break before you can choose another song. Either way, you are saving money!
- If you regularly purchase movies digitally, then you should consider subscribing to a streaming service such as Netflix or Hulu. Hulu also has a free version which has a great selection of films and television shows. Again, if you do not have a need to view a film or television program

digitally, see if your local library has DVDs in stock.

- For e-books, there are many digital libraries which allow you to "borrow" an e-book for a limited time, just as you would borrow a physical book at a library. I can even look into an e-book subscription service and purchase a large number of books for a monthly fee; if you purchase several e-books, this is sure to be a more cost-efficient solution. With audiobooks, there are services such as Audible that allow you one free book per month for a monthly fee. Plus, the subscription fee includes a discount on any additional books. This is something to look into if you purchase audiobooks regularly. Also, if you want an audiobook for a book in the public domain (meaning that its copyright has expired) check out www.Librivox.org or similar websites. These websites have audiobooks for thousands of books in the public domain from Aesop's Fables to the works of Geoffrey Chaucer.

- Apps and software can be tricky. There are so many that are free which we download impulsively. As I have already said, ensure that you clean your devices of any unnecessary apps and software. But what about ones that you paid for? There are two alternatives to this problem. If there is an app or software you wish to purchase, then you must *first* look for a free alternative. Ask yourself, "Do I need to purchase an app for filming videos on my phone, or is the in-built app sufficient?" This leads to the second solution: asking yourself if you really need the app. Using the same example, there are many fantastic apps which enhance the quality of the videos you shoot on your phone. These apps have been used to shoot feature films! But if you are not a filmmaker or you do not have an inherent need to create cinema quality videos, then there is no need to purchase this app. Save your money so that you can afford the *freedom* to do something else!

- If you are going to purchase a game, then I hope you will find time to play it! Ensure that you will spend time to play this game. You do not need to become a full-time gamer, but what is the point of purchasing a game if you will never play it? Also, there is a difference in purchasing a video game and purchasing a quick game to enjoy on your phone. The games made for our phones are used to fill empty time – perhaps during our lunch break or on our daily commute. If this is why you play games on your phone, then look for free games which will occupy your time and are enjoyable to play. Also, look for other ways to fill in empty time –

there was a time when we did not need to bury our faces in our phones to enjoy moments of inactivity!

This is the minimalist approach to our digital purchases. Look for these alternatives to save your money on digital purchases and to cut back on your digital usage. Minimizing your digital usage will maximize your quality of life.

Time And Time Again...

Time is of the essence! The main focus and agenda behind embracing the minimalist lifestyle is to ensure you have more time and freedom to pursue what you wish in life. Time and freedom will ensure you live your best life. It is only when time is taken from us that we begin to value it and its importance in our lives. Once you have time on your side, or if you have already had it, it is easy to slip away from minimalism and fall into the trap of consumerism, endangering your time and freedom. Many individuals adopt minimalism once they realize their time and freedom have been taken away from them. So far, you have learned how a simple action like a small purchase can affect your time and freedom at a later stage. This is why managing and evaluating your time is a crucial aspect of becoming a minimalist.

It is time to grab your notebook and pen once again! Here is what I want you to write down:

- What time and freedom have you already lost? Have you missed out on events, holidays, important long-term purchases?
- What time and freedom have you gained due to minimalism? Reflect once again on a minimalist action you took which reaped its rewards: for example, you may write about spending less on material goods and as a result you went on that cruise to The Bahamas!

Now, I want you to analyze your time. Ideally you will spend the majority of your time on leisure, but this is not always practical. Work, school, and the responsibilities of life will most likely take precedent – they will most likely take up a significant portion of your time. However, you must ensure that they are not taking all of your time and that you have a decent amount of time which is being spent on what you wish to spend it on!

Keep your notebook and pen by your side. On a blank page, write "Time Log" at the top, with the date next to it. Record a day from your week in the Time Log. Record how much time is spent on work, school, and responsibilities. You can record it as follows:

- Gym from 6 AM to 7 PM (1 Hour)

- Breakfast with friend from 7:30 AM to 8:30 AM (1 Hour)
- Work from 9 AM to 5 PM (8 Hours)
- Studying and attending class from 7 PM to 9 PM (2 Hours)
- Chores – various times during the day. (Total accumulation: 1 Hour)
- Catching up on my favorite television show 10 PM to 11 PM (1 Hour)

Your total time of activity on this day was 14 Hours. 10 Hours were to spare on which some time would obviously be spent on sleep. If you sleep for 8 hours, you have 2 hours to spare. This may be scattered over the course of a day and may not be an uninterrupted 2 hours. But what are you doing during those 2 hours? The above example shows that work, studying, and chores take up the majority of your time. While this may be inevitable, the short amount of time to enjoy what you truly want is limited. Would you have time for a longer gym session? Instead of simply having breakfast with your friend, could you spend an entire day with them? And catching up on your favorite television show? I am sure you would rather binge-watch it!

Let us look at studying and attending class first. You may be required to attend an in-person class, but if you are a university student or are attending a professional development course, see if there are alternatives to take these classes online. This way you will have more flexibility to complete your course and will not be obligated to sit in a lecture hall for a set time. With studying, see if there are methods that can allow you to study in a more efficient manner. This way studying will take up less of your time without compromising your performance on a project or exam. If studying involves a lot of reading, here are a few methods that you can follow to understand the text more efficiently:

- Take a speed-reading course; this will not only teach you to read faster, but to absorb the knowledge quicker.

- See if there are any summarized notes for your text. If you are required to read a novel for a course, see if there are online notes or publications which summarize the key points of the novel. The more well-known the novel is, the greater the chance.

- Listening instead of reading! If your text is available as an audiobook, this may be a more efficient way to understand it. Plus, it is easier to revisit a certain section via audio than to keep turning back pages in a book.

- Find a study group. If you study with others and bounce ideas of each other, you should grasp the text quicker and therefore *minimize* the amount of self-study you would have to do for your best performance.

Now what about those annoying chores, errands, and responsibilities we all have thrown at us? They seem to get in the way of our work and studying, let alone enjoying our leisure time. What can we do to minimize our time spent on these necessities and therefore maximize our time on our leisurely activities?

These requirements will change constantly, but take a moment to jot down what chores, errands, and responsibilities you have to tackle on a daily basis. Here is an example:

- Drop children off at school in the morning; pick them up in the afternoon.
- Ensure that bills are paid and there are no outstanding or overdue charges.
- Ensure that laundry is done and that there are sufficient clothes for the following day.
- Ensure that there is sufficient food to eat for the day.

Now let us use minimalism to tackle these activities and maximize our time.

- Continue to drop off the children at school in the morning and pick them up in the afternoon. No change should happen here if you can help it. If you really need an alternative, see if there are carpooling options or a school bus or any other method of public transportation which takes them to and from school.

- To alleviate the hassle of continuously checking the bills to see if they need paying, see if you can set up an automatic payment schedule for the bills. Of course, ensure that you have sufficient funds at all times! Many automatic payment systems will inform you that your bill will be charged soon, so you will have time to make any changes if necessary.

- Now, if you are a minimalist, you should have a more modest wardrobe and therefore might need to do laundry more often than if you had a closet stuffed full of clothes. Often the most convenient time to wash and dry clothes is at night so that they are ready in the morning. For ironing, see if you can allocate time during the night or early morning or during leisure time.

- See if you can prepare food in advance. If you prepare food in bulk, it will minimize or completely eliminate the need for cooking during the week.

Taking these small steps should free up your time during your week. These are all minimalist efforts toward maximizing your time. Now what about the big one? Work!

Work

Reducing the amount of time you work is a difficult challenge and you may not be able to do so. But if you are able to free up other areas of your life and make space for leisure, work will not feel overwhelming. Here are things to consider if you are able to reduce the amount of time dedicated to your job:

- Do you need to work the number of hours you do? Are you choosing to work this number of hours? Are you working additional hours to pay off debt?
- Are you willing to change your job or career to find one that suits your schedule, *even if it means a lower salary?*
- Are you overworking yourself for a possible promotion or for the sake of maintaining an identity?

Are you only required to work a certain number of hours per week? Maybe the answer is yes, and you are voluntarily choosing to work longer hours. You do not need to pay off any debt and you have more than sufficient funds to pay your bills. What are you working for then? If you are saving up for a purchase, it is time to go back and analyze the upcoming purchase.

Is the purchase worth it? If you are purchasing a new house for your family, then I would say yes. Same for a car, if you need a car for regular transportation. Or perhaps the money is being earned to invest later. If you are working additional hours to go on holiday, it is worth it! But are you saving up for material items that are disposable? Or to earn enough to have a budget for Black Friday as well as holiday shopping? It is not worth the extra hours – reduce your time at work. Even if the purchase is worth it, you should ensure that after the purchase is made you are able to reduce your work time to *enjoy* the purchase. If these additional hours are to pay off your debt, then keep working! But ensure that once your debt is paid off you take time off. After all, you are aiming to be debt free so that you can have more time and freedom for yourself.

But what if you are unable to lower the number of hours you work? Perhaps you are required to work a set number of hours; perhaps you are expected to work overtime and there is no chance of having your hours reduced. Are you willing to change your position? What about changing to another company which will allow you to work a lesser number of hours? Or what about finding another job in another field, even if it calls for a reduction of salary? Or even taking the biggest leap and starting your own business? These are difficult decisions and if you are considering any one of them, I implore you to take your time and weigh the pros and cons of the decisions.

Changing your current position within your company may offer a lesser number of hours, yet it may not be in a department you particularly enjoy or are skilled at. Taking on a new position, job, or career may guarantee you a lesser number of hours, but if it brings a lower salary it may cause additional issues: maybe it will be more difficult to pay your bills, pay off your debt, or make meaningful purchases. You may have more time for leisure, but you may not have the money for certain leisurely activities – maybe that holiday will have to be postponed indefinitely. If you have dependents, this is particularly difficult – you would not want to deprive them of anything due to a lesser salary.

There are minimalists who have opted for a career change with a lower salary and have found it beneficial. While you may no longer earn the income for certain things, if you are diligently following the minimalist lifestyle, you may not *need* the additional income. Maybe everything you need is covered by your new salary – plus, you now have time to enjoy these things.

What about aiming for the promotion? Promotions and "moving up the ladder" always seem like the next logical step. We are told we must always step out of our comfort zone and therefore always aim for the next best thing, keep our options open, and never stop moving. But this is the trap we fall into and it is strikingly similar to our falling prey to consumerism. Use the minimalist approach toward working for a promotion – think about what this promotion will bring you. Most likely it will bring you more prestige, a higher status, and a higher salary. But is it also bringing you more time and more freedom? Think carefully about why you are working additional hours and whether a possible promotion is worth it if it will not improve your quality of life.

Another reason we desire to work more or earn a promotion is because of *status*. There is no difference between our consuming and hoarding of material goods and our desire to keep up appearances by overworking. Our culture and our society would like us to portray an image that we are hardworking and busy. Having free time is looked upon with guilt – when we say, "They have too much time on their hands," it is an *insult* rather than a *compliment*!

But you are a minimalist! You have the goal to live *more with less*. While others may not understand your actions and decisions, you should not work more simply to keep up a status. You are not a minimalist to impress others; you are a minimalist to live a better life for yourself. Do not forget this!

Remaining Minimalist

As a final note, I wish to stress the dangers of falling out of the minimalist mindset and being sucked in by consumerism – leading to reckless spending and careless living. Take a moment to think about why you decided to read this book and learn about minimalism. In fact, take out your notebook one more time and make a list (as short or as long as you would like) on why you decided to learn about minimalism. Here are some common reasons, and I am sure some, many, or all of these reasons apply to you:

- Simplifying your life
- Spending less and saving your money
- Paying off debt
- Living a more focused and deliberate life
- Eradicating physical and digital clutter

Now here is a tricky exercise. Underneath your reasons for wishing to learn about minimalism, write down a list of what prevented you from becoming a minimalist sooner. Ask yourself, *why did I have these habits before – the habits that are the antithesis of minimalism?*

Here are some of the reasons why many people are NOT minimalists:

- Addiction to consuming – be it material goods, food, drugs, etc.
- Possessing a feeling that consumption brings happiness and improves quality of life
- Societal expectations

When you compare your two lists, see what has changed and what still needs to change – if anything. Perhaps you were addicted to consuming and now that has been alleviated. Do you still at times feel you would be happier if you owned more things? minimalism does not happen overnight; it may take time for habits and feelings to develop. Do not be in rush. If you practice the exercises mentioned in this book, *it will happen.*

What about societal expectations? This might be the biggest reason as to why people are not minimalists, even if they have an innate desire to adopt the lifestyle. I wanted to save this thought for last, as this is something to ponder when you observe your journey toward adopting the minimalist lifestyle.

Many individuals who live in the most developed and richest nations in the world fall prey to consumerism due to societal pressures. Often, many of the richest nations will project their greatness by showing what its inhabitants own and can own. Many individuals in these nations will be reminded of their privilege by being fed with images and statistics of individuals in lesser-developed nations. Images of children without shoes are shown, or photos of the modest living quarters for families, or people walking long distances because they have no access to vehicles. This creates the mindset that because of our possessions and our access to more possessions, we have a higher status in life. This mentality weighs on our shoulders throughout our lives. To showcase our success in life we must have a bigger home, a fancier car, and a range of possessions from designer clothing to antique furniture to books we will never read but are bestsellers and thereby an exhibition of our intellect. Living up to this ideal is a societal pressure and is why we do not live measured and deliberate lives, which is what the basis of the minimalist lifestyle is founded upon.

But what about individuals in so-called developing nations? You may not think it, but they are experiencing the same societal pressure that those in "First World" nations face. Their economies are growing and, as a result, income for these inhabitants is increasing tremendously. To celebrate this newly gained income, inhabitants of developing nations are consuming. For the first time, they are wearing designer clothing, perhaps purchasing their first car or upgrading their current automobile to something more luxurious. Empty spaces in their homes are filled within a short span of time – apparently due to a newly found, almost sudden appreciation for painting and sculpture. Due to the fast-paced consumption they are faced with, they may feel that life is getting better and that they are happier. They may as well be! After all, they are not deprived of things as they may have been before. But sooner or later, they will realize that possessions are not bringing them true happiness. A wave of minimalism may well appear in these nations in the coming years.

You Don't Have To Work *That* Hard...

Many of us have been raised with the outlook of having to work more to earn more. We are taught that working hard is of the utmost importance. Yet, working *smartly* is vastly underrated. Minimalism does not want to make money the central focus of your life but realizes that it is an important aspect of life and therefore continuous high-earning and a high income is a necessity for many individuals. If you fall under the bracket of needing to earn more income to sustain a particular lifestyle or to help your dependents, there may be methods for you to minimize your work without having to minimize your financial gains. Here are a few:

- Get help for your work. This may sound contradictory to the do-it-yourself lifestyle which was mentioned before; but remember, this is specifically for your job. Are there tasks which can be delegated to others? You may be spending money doing this which seems counter-productive but perhaps can increase productivity; the work completed may increase and therefore, financial gains may come. For example, if you need some writing work completed, there are many websites such as Fiverr.com where for a fee as low as $5 you can have these services completed. It is not a lot of money, and you will have a skilled professional who may do a better job than you can, so you end up reaping greater rewards.

- Automation! Obviously, automation does not work for every job, but perhaps there are steps you can take to automate certain aspects of your job. The process for automation may be lengthy, but it has a great trade-off. Many Internet entrepreneurs will launch a product and program it so that Artificial Intelligence manages the work that a human would otherwise do. Their work decreases significantly, and the product continues to bring them profit. See if there is something with your job you can automate.

- Ensure you are as knowledgeable as can be in other departments of your job, to maximize efficiency. This is especially vital if you own a business. One department within your business may be intentionally completing their work on a longer basis and therefore may be unfairly charging you extra; you may be able to find a more efficient method to complete the work.

- Have multiple sources of income. How often have you heard someone say, "I want to do this, but I will not make a lot of money!" or "I want to be this, but sadly I will not earn a lot of money!" But who says your primary occupation has to be your only source of income in your life? Do your research on how you can develop multiple streams of income – by having a side job, doing odd-jobs that you are skilled in, investing your money, etc. Do not feel that the limits of your profession should limit your financial freedom.

It is crucial for human beings to find and utilize free time to reflect on what means the most to us. Do not forget that this book is about adopting a minimalist lifestyle; it has discussed how to get rid of possessions, how to save money, and manage one's finances. But the bigger picture behind these tasks is to live a meaningful life. It is deliberate, meaningful, and happy living that form the criterion for an excellent quality of life. Keep this in mind during your continuous journey with minimalism.

It's time for another reflection exercise; go ahead and grab your notebook and pen once again and answer the following questions in as much detail as possible:

- Why did you decide to purchase this book and learn about minimalism? (I know this has been asked before, but your viewpoint will continuously change as you progress in your journey.)
- What steps did you take to become minimalist?
- What steps were the easiest to undertake?
- What steps were the hardest to undertake?
- What steps do you still need to take to continue as a minimalist?
- Are there any steps which you feel you cannot or refuse to take?
- What reactions did others have when you announced you were embracing the minimalist

lifestyle? Did you have any detractors? Did you defend yourself and how so?

- What has been the best part of becoming a minimalist?
- What has been the worst part of becoming a minimalist?

This may seem lengthy and unnecessary now that you are toward the end of this book, but I would like you to focus extensively on these questions and revisit them from time to time. Maybe create a schedule of every month or every three months when you will revisit the questions and answer them again.

Chapter Summary

- The digital world takes up much of our time, but it does not have to be this way.
- A great minimalist knows a thing or two about time management.
- Make your job work around your schedule; your schedule should not work around your job.

In the next chapter, you will learn about quality of life, and how it ties into minimalism.

Chapter Six: Quality Of Life

In this chapter, you will learn about quality of life, and why you should value peace of mind.

We all give in to our hearts desires, do we not? Regardless of our current context or the environment we were raised in, we feel a strong sense of discontent. We all have desires to achieve something; and perhaps even greater desires to *attain* something. This is what leads us to consume. We grew up not having a certain thing, and now that we can afford to purchase it, we do not think twice about purchasing it.

Our desires and our standards of living continue to change, and for most of us continue to increase. We desire to have a job with a particular salary and convince ourselves that once we reach this milestone our life is set and there is nothing more that we need. However, as our standard of living improves, we become accustomed to it. Eventually, we begin to grow out of it. We were never too pleased with the environment in which we were raised, regardless of how privileged it may or may not have been; as a result, we desired more. The same occurs with our standard of living: we begin to feel it is insufficient and therefore, we desire more. Progress is a good word – yet we do not seem to truly understand what progress means. While we should aim for a high standard of living, we should not confuse this with quality of life.

What is quality of life? You have read the phrase several times in this book. But before you continue on with your minimalist journey, I would like you to have a true understanding of what it means. Quality of life describes the satisfaction a human being feels in their lifetime. The positives in their life outweighs the negatives, and they generally feel a sense of contentment and happiness. Our progress has become defined by our acquisition of material goods; and we are so engulfed in our pursuit of these goods that we convince ourselves that no matter how much we may already have, we are still deprived of what is best for us.

The saddest part is, that once we acquire these material goods, we often lose what already was bringing us happiness. To maintain our new lifestyles, we have to work tirelessly, often sacrificing more pleasurable activities so that we do not lose an opportunity to grow our income. Before we know it, our lives are preoccupied with *pursuing* happiness rather than *being* happy and doing the things we love, with the people whom we love. This is the trap which many of us have fallen into, and the tragedy is that many of us realize at a late stage. But I want to assure you, that it is *never* too late for a change.

You will recall that one of the preconceived notions about minimalism is that the lifestyle is only for a particular demographic – of which one of the criteria is that an individual has to be of a certain age to pursue the lifestyle. Regardless of your age, or what stage in life you are in, you can adopt the minimalist lifestyle if you would like to. You may receive backlash – but most of it will be misunderstanding. Your stating a desire to become minimalist will turn heads, with many thinking you wish to become as ascetic. Be patient and do not stress yourself trying to convince them that what you are doing is correct – do not attempt to proselytize either; remember that minimalism is not a religion.

You are doing this for yourself. You are aware of your current lifestyle, and you possess a desire to live with more awareness and to live *deliberately*. That is why you decided to take the leap and approach your life through the philosophy of minimalism. As an idea and as a way of life, minimalism is centuries old; it has found itself in various forms in a plethora of cultures from East to West. One thing that is found throughout different schools of minimalism is a certain set of principles deemed fit for a peaceful life. Peace of mind should be an aim for all humans, and self-help is on the rise because of a lack of peace of mind. The newly sparked interest in minimalism has also developed due to the population having a stressful life, and having difficulty finding peace of mind. You have learned about trade-offs: should you purchase this item? What will be the trade-off? Will you still have *time* and *freedom* if you purchase a material good?

As a final exercise, take out your notebook – tear out a page (you may need more than one) – and answer these questions in as much details as possible:

- Prior to beginning your journey with minimalism, what were three of the most peaceful and happy moments of your life? Detail these events as much as possible.
- Prior to beginning your journey with minimalism, what were three of the most pleasurable moments of your life? Detail these events as much as possible.
- Prior to beginning your journey with minimalism, what were three of the most painful moments of your life? Detail these events as much as possible.

Once these have been written, place them on your wall. You can tape them, stick them, etc., just ensure that your writing is clearly visible on a wall you regularly see on a daily basis. You have to endeavor to achieve that your trade-offs will lead to peace of mind and to pleasure; and that it will not lead you to pain. Let us look back at the

"If…then" statements. Now that you have mastered this strategy, it is time to apply three conditions to *then*. After asking the *if*, ask yourself "Will the *then* provide me with peace, pleasure, or pain?"

Ideally, you will receive peace and pleasure simultaneously. This may not always happen, but you should aim as often as you can for peace. With sustained peace of mind, pleasure will come naturally. However, pleasure may not always lead to peace of mind, and may often lead to pain. After all, consumerism *does* give us pleasure. We do feel an instant gratification when we purchase a material good we worked so hard at our job to earn. We anticipate the gifts we will receive for our birthdays or for a holiday celebration, and we do feel ecstatic when we receive the gift of our choice.

But eventually, none of these material goods bring us peace of mind; the pleasure wears off and we may, in fact, feel a great deal of pain from possessing the material good. The same could be true for our dream career. We often think that if we are able to acquire all we desire, then we have achieved happiness. We feel that we are downtrodden if we do not receive everything that we desire, or that we have worked hard for. But here is a crazy idea: maybe not receiving everything we want is true freedom.

While I do not want you to lose your ambition or to feel that you must be content at all times – you should not base your contentment on conditions. Whether you succeed or fail in a goal, you should feel a sense of contentment. If you have your peace of mind and can enjoy life's pleasures, then it is without doubt that you have achieved freedom. Do your best to maintain this. This should be the goal of minimalism, and I am certain that after following the exercises in this book you will be able to achieve what you truly desire in life. Your mindset will change, and you will live life with a great consciousness. Your life will not be controlled by possessions, and you will value all of the possessions you do own and that you will own in the future.

What you have accomplished so far is a major step. Do not worry if you feel there is much more to attain. Your achievements thus far show promise; you have displayed a strong sense of commitment, and you should have no problem in continuing on your journey as a minimalist. Embracing the minimalist lifestyle is an intimidating change, but you have shown tremendous courage and I wish you well in your endeavors.

Chapter Summary

- We are so focused on improving our standard of living that we disregard the quality of life.
- Do not undervalue peace of mind.

Strive so that your actions provide you with peace of mind and pleasure.

Final Words

Thanks again for taking the time to purchase this book!

You should now have a good understanding of minimalist living and be able to budget accordingly to maintain a minimalist lifestyle, learn to be more frugal with your spending, and live your best life without needing material things!

If you enjoyed this book, please take the time to leave me a review on Amazon. I appreciate your honest feedback, and it really helps me to continue producing high quality books.

An Afterthought...

What you have accomplished and what you will continue to accomplish as a minimalist is no easy feat; letting go and admiring simplicity is a challenge in our fast-paced, high-pressure, and consumerist culture. But no matter how you feel, remember that you are doing a great service to yourself. Even in moments of doubt, I am sure you will be glad you embraced the minimalist lifestyle. Minimalism is here to stay and will continue to surge in popularity as the desire to focus on the important things in life becomes paramount once again.

There is so much more I can say about minimalism, but you will learn more as you continue on your journey. And perhaps there is no need for me to elaborate any further.

After all, less is more.